"Exploring the Earth and Beyond"
Funding for this item provided by a
Library Services and Technology (LSTA)
Grant made possible by the Illinois
State Library - 2013

Asian Animals

Camels

by Lyn A. Sirota

Consulting Editor: Gail Saunders-Smith, PhD

Content Consultant: Tanya Dewey, PhD
University of Michigan Museum of Zoology

CAPSTONE PRESS
a capstone imprint

Pebble Plus is published by Capstone Press,
1710 Roe Crest Drive, North Mankato, Minnesota 56003.
www.capstonepub.com

 Books published by Capstone Press are manufactured with paper
containing at least 10 percent post-consumer waste.

Library of Congress Cataloging-in-Publication Data
Sirota, Lyn A., 1963–
    Camels / by Lyn A. Sirota.
    p. cm. — (Pebble plus. Asian animals)
    Summary: "Simple text and photographs present Bactrian camels, how they look, where they live, and what
they do" — Provided by publisher.
    Includes bibliographical references and index.
    ISBN 978-1-4296-3992-7 (library binding)
    ISBN 978-1-4296-4844-8 (paperback)
    1. Camels — Juvenile literature. I. Title.
QL737.U54S57 2010
599.63'62 — dc22   2009028641

Editorial Credits
Katy Kudela, editor; Matt Bruning, designer; Svetlana Zhurkin, media researcher; Eric Manske, production specialist

Photo Credits
Alamy/Arco Images GmbH, 15; Alamy/Marcus Wilson-Smith, 7; iStockphoto/David Kerkhoff, 1; iStockphoto/Keith
Molloy, 21; Minden Pictures/Colin Monteath, 17; Minden Pictures/Gertrud & Helmut Denzau, 11; Peter Arnold/
Biosphoto/Michel Gunther, cover; Shutterstock/Dmitry Pichugin, 9; Shutterstock/Elimoe, 5; Shutterstock/Noo, 19;
Shutterstock/sad, 13

Note to Parents and Teachers

The Asian Animals series supports national science standards related to life science.
This book describes and illustrates Bactrian camels. The images support early readers in
understanding the text. The repetition of words and phrases helps early readers learn new
words. This book also introduces early readers to subject-specific vocabulary words, which are
defined in the Glossary section. Early readers may need assistance to read some words and to
use the Table of Contents, Glossary, Read More, Internet Sites, and Index sections of the book.

Printed in the United States of America in North Mankato, Minnesota.
062013
007381R

Table of Contents

Living in Asia

Bactrian camels travel
the grasslands and
rocky deserts of Asia.
They live in places that are
blazing hot and icy cold.

World Map

North America

Europe

Asia

Africa

South America

Australia

Antarctica

Bactrian camels live in
Mongolia and China.
People use tame camels
to carry heavy loads.
Wild herds live in the deserts.

where Bactrian camels live

Up Close!

Camels have long legs.

They step through sand

on their wide, padded feet.

When the wind blows,

a camel closes its nostrils

to keep out sand.

Long eyelashes block sand

from its eyes.

Bactrian camels have

two humps on their backs.

They store fat in their humps.

They live on the fat

when food is hard to find.

Eating and Drinking

Camels eat grass and plants.

They have tough

mouths and stomachs.

They even eat thorns.

Camels drink

from rivers, streams,

and mountain springs.

They drink salty water too.

Staying Safe

Hungry wolves hunt
young or sick camels.
Camels must watch
and listen for danger.

Wild camels are endangered.

To help save them,

people are protecting land

for wild camels to graze.

Glossary

endangered — in danger of dying out

eyelash — one of the short, curved hairs that grows on the edge of eyelids

graze — to eat grass and plants growing in a field

hump — the rounded area on the back of a camel; Bactrian camels have two humps.

nostril — two openings in the nose through which animals breathe and smell

pad — the soft part on the bottom of the feet of some animals

protect — to keep safe

tame — taken from the wild and trained to live with or be useful to people

thorn — a sharp point on the branch or stem of a plant

Read More

Lindeen, Carol K. *Life in a Desert.* Living in a Biome. Mankato, Minn.: Capstone Press, 2004.

Ripple, William John. *Camels.* Desert Animals. Mankato, Minn.: Capstone Press, 2005.

Stevens, Kathryn. *Camels.* New Naturebooks. Mankato, Minn.: Child's World, 2008.

Internet Sites

FactHound offers a safe, fun way to find Internet sites related to this book. All of the sites on FactHound have been researched by our staff.

Here's all you do:

Visit *www.facthound.com*

FactHound will fetch the best sites for you!

Index

Word Count: 159
Grade: 1
Early-Intervention Level: 18